Crossing Point
Modern American Poetry

HEARTLAND

Mariela Griffor

ARS INTERPRES PUBLICATIONS

HEARTLAND
Mariela Griffor

Copyright © 2010 by Ars Interpres Publications
Copyright © 2010 by Mariela Griffor

Cover Design and Illustrations by

Published by Ars Interpres Publications

www.arsint.com

Printed in Stockholm by Författares Bokmaskin 2010

ISBN 978-91-85931-11-8

CONTENTS

PROLOGUE	8
LOVE FOR A SUBVERSIVE MAN	9
SUNDAY WALK, URBAN TALK	11
THE RAIN	13
CHILD'S EYES	15
HEARTLAND	16
TO JULIO SANTIBÁÑEZ (1960-1985)	18
QUIXOTE AS A DREAM	19
RED ROBIN	20
SELECTIVE EXPOSURE	22
PARADE	24
AMNESIA	26
DO YOU REMEMBER LOVE?	27
HAIR OF SAND	28
THE MOMENT OF TRUTH	29
LOVE IN TIME OF WAR	31
THE DEW	32
JEALOUS STATE	33
UNEXPECTED DEATH	34
BOYS	36
MEN OF FLESH AND BLOOD	38
LOSS	39
CHRISTMAS	40
PRAYER	41
WHAT A SHAME	42
SAFE CONDUCT	43
RETURN	45
SUNSPOTS	46
ALONG THE COLD STREETS OF SCANDINAVIA	47
HUSBAND	49
DEATH POSTPONED	50
WOLF	51
HOW CHAOS BEGINS	53
OLD MOUNTAINS	54
SONG FOR CHILE	55
RIPPLES	57
VALENTINE'S DAY IN DETROIT	58
CYANIDE SMILE	59
INSOMNIA	60
GREED	61

SOMETIMES	62
ABSOLUTION	63
BROKEN GLASS	64
TWINKIES	65
ARCADE	66
FROM THE GRAVES OF LATIN AMERICA	67
DETROIT	68

For

J.S (1960-1985)
R.I.V.P (1956-1987)
M.A.B (1959-1991)
J.N (1956-1987)

PROLOGUE

Out here, the snow is an insider,
it's the haute couture of my days.
I invent a friend to pour out
remembrances of the old country.

Out here, I invent new sounds, new men, new women.
I assassinate the old days with nostalgia.
I don't see but invent a city and its people, its fury, its sky.

I don't belong to the earth but to the air.
As I invent you, I invent myself.

LOVE FOR A SUBVERSIVE MAN

I

What do we do with the love
if you die?
Do we put it in your coffin
together with the green, red and gray plaid shirt
you like so much?
With your khaki pants
and light brown shoes,
the ones you use in your normal life?
Or do we wrap it around
the flag the Patriotic Front militia
will bring to cover you?

I spend nights sleepless
thinking about what to do
with the love if you die.

Maybe we could put it
in a crown of flowers
like the ones people weave
for Scandinavian men
when they become bridegrooms.

Your mother would say: "No!
Chilean men don't wear flowers on their heads."
It would be awkward.
I understand her.

I would try to put it
in a letter that you
could read when you are alone
and lonesome.

To be honest
I don't know what to do
with the love if you die.

II

Santiago is a scarlet puddle
of idiots,
poets,
assassins, and
innocents.
You said it yourself
before it happened.

III

I remember only the
scars over your lips,
scars over your left eyebrow,
the pieces of flesh missing
around your nostrils.

The pain of your scars
wakes me up at night and I hurt
as I did giving birth to your child.

I don't know with any certainty
what to do next.

One day at a time they tell me.

I will wait until the answer
comes with clarity from
behind the smoke of the landmine
or the hand grenade that took you
away from my hand.

I will keep secret all your names,
the places where
we will raise barricades and mount
attacks on police stations
until they kill us all

or they surrender.

SUNDAY WALK, URBAN TALK

For Recaredo Ignacio Valenzuela

Since our conversation about Guevara failed,
nothing was going to be prolific
that Sunday.
Except small disagreements on this
and that.

We walked towards the gates of
O'Higgins Park, where we trained
among Santiaguinos, ice-cream parlours,
handicraft stores and armed police here
and there.

Every Sunday we entered the
park pretending to be a couple,
jogging our way away from a nightmare,
pretending you were "George" and I was "Rebecca".

In those days we didn't need much.
    a heavy ammunition was resting in our hearts.

None of us wanted to be compared with Guevara.
Too tiring. Too much. Almost sacrilege.
Not for what people think.
None of us wanted to leave the country
or experience any adventures.

You wanted to go to your classes,
teach year after year,
come back in the evenings
and find a woman who liked you
as much as you liked her.

Myself, I wanted a garden,
big, full of plants and eccentric flowers,
read the newspapers in the morning,
write a bit about things I couldn't say

and love "Philip" as always.

Ignacio, what happened?
We were almost sure we would make it out alive.

What kind of country is this
that falls in love with death
every time freedom disappears
from its core?

What kind of country is this
that kills its own sons and daughters?

Somebody will have to wash away your blood
from Alhue Street
and the river of blood on Pedro Donoso.

Someday, somebody
has to do something with it.

THE RAIN

The sound of the rain in Michigan
reminds me of the rugged winters in my old country:
the cold feet in old shoes,
the fast sound of the water hitting the ground,
the smell of eucalyptus in the air.
I close my eyes and make a wish:
Wish I could see, for just a moment, your hair
dancing over your face
trying to escape the weather.
I wish I could see again your hands looking
for a warm, soft place as a shelter in my body.
I wish the rain would never stop.

I open my eyes and know I am here
listening without you.
The clock from the dining room tells me it
is past midnight,
the rain still plays in the garden and on
the streets of Detroit
washing away disillusionment, bad thoughts,
cleansing the sirens of the police cars,
washing little by little the fear of
new encounters and new violent truths.
I move silently through the rooms of my house,
if I make a mistake
the children will come to me at a
gallop and my affair with the rain
will stop.

The clock shows me its hand again
and the rain is still raining.
I close my eyes and make another wish:
you and I sitting on the rocks of
El Yeco, late at night or early
morning, waiting always for the light,
waiting for the good things the rain will bring
back to us. You extend your hand and say:
Look! Make a wish. There's a rainbow.

And in a single movement we braid our
hands and dream dreams, both at the same time,
so we can keep it secret, and holy,
until death parts us.

CHILD'S EYES

People say that children see and hear things
they themselves cannot see or hear,
and this child breaking into
the room to hug and kiss
his grandmother, Wilma,
hasn't seen me yet.
I am afraid of his eyes,
touching like a hummingbird
the cornea of my eyes.
I don't want him to see
the puddle of
old pain and rusty love
that grows inside me,
the spider web of my disappointment,
a beaten heart that
has never overcome the loss of him.
I am afraid of this child
running around with his two frank
years, afraid of me breaking.
I'm sure he would scream
if I let my pupils touch his,
and the room would look
at me knowing the truth of
what he sees.
I am afraid and old,
smashing day after day
a memory of innocence.
I know too much.
My mind is futile.

HEARTLAND

I wish I could put my heart
under the faucet in the sink
and with the running water
wash away the thumping
thoughts you evoke.

Who would guess that day I
saw you walking through the
long corridor in that strange country
that you would stay in my mind until this day,
that there is not more of you
than these memories.

Thoughts of washing away
nostalgias and melancholies
jump into my brain,
as if water can
cure all our pains.

After years of draining
the arteries of my
heart, they come full
again every morning as our first encounter,
insisting on the memory of you.

What can be more tragic than to die young?
The death of someone younger, maybe,
or the indifference of a people to such deaths.

How can we continue this way
to meet our gods if
our loved ones left us before?
Little consolation in knowing
there is no escape from death,
and as you sleep in your grave,
I will join you
someday.

It is not the regret of not having been
able to love you more or deeper, or not
having said the unsaid, it is not
the regret of not having been better to you or
the others that I loved.
It is the certainty
that nothing can conquer
death and its humiliation
that bothers me today.

TO JULIO SANTIBÁÑEZ (1960-1985)

I would have liked to offer you verses,
embroidered with the petals of Chilean roses.
That has not been possible.
This time my verses have poured out years of pain for having
lost you.
I have mended in these lost years day by day my broken heart,
and risen little by little from the ground to talk to you.
The time has passed slowly like the river in summer.
Still I remember how you were and still you are latent
and alive in my embrace.
I remember you quiet and distant,
good and wise in the memories of your friends,
beautiful and healthy, a born dreamer and proud.
I remember you my love
on this road of blessings, along this solitary journey.
I would have liked to offer you flowers and pomegranates from
the past.
That has not been possible.
I would like to rest my wounds and let the cries escape,
waiting for some miracle.

QUIXOTE AS A DREAM

Galloping between mountains and valleys
his beard of wind moves,
his iron helmet,
his thin body,
his wrinkle of genius,
he moves with the leaps of the horse.

allied in white with the universe,
whose dream has brought
the mantle with which
Spain covers its body,
spaces that fill all
when we seek
grace and balance.

Where does our knight
start this endless search
that converts him into
a hero for those without dreams?

Galloping between mountains and valleys
its mantle of pride moves
its beard of wind
hurrying its step as we go
all of us running
to meet him.

RED ROBIN

For Robin Gandy

*The numberless heart of the wind
beating above our loving silence.*

Pablo Neruda

How is it that after so many years
people are still talking about you?

Their envy
pulsates in their throats and temples,
creeps into their days,
scratches with long nails
their hearts and minds.

The first time I heard your laugh
I jumped, surprised.
It reminded me of the way
a beggar laughs in children's tales:
smoky and loud.

The entire
room looked back to you
and became a subtle dance
around your fingers.

The mathematicians there,
an obscure Stoltenberg and
a forever unknown Palmgren,
could not figure out
how a man as rebellious
and provocative toward the establishment
could enter a room and be King.
Is science always concerned with killing our illusions?
They took the smoke of your
pipe as an insult. Swedish
men cannot smoke pipes.

It is too expensive.

You didn't know they talked behind your back.
I'm here to tell you
so you know what to do with them.

The party was proper,
just a single moment
of farewell to their decadence.
The food was tasty
and the wine, as always, ran.

My friend and I ended up
doing dishes while all of you
discussed numbers about which we didn't care.

After you left, their comments:
your affair with Turing
your failure to follow in his footsteps.
Their throats and temples pulsating again.
They didn't want anything else
than to be in your shoes.

Who really cares about them?
Who will be remembered of them and their
work or their love stories?
After his suicide Turing left
all his papers to you, his student.

They didn't understand pre-cosmic
catastrophes or greatness or success.

He got his cure for death
and you got more love than you could handle.

Turing's heart was certainly well placed.
It is bad luck you couldn't see that in time.

SELECTIVE EXPOSURE

In Detroit it is easy to see pheasants walking the alleys,
or children running like a flock hunting a dog,
murals of Jesus, Martin Luther King, Bob Marley
or B.B. King on dirty walls,
pink, velvet sofas covered by bags full of garbage,
falling sheer to the streets.
Sometimes old garages are semi-fallen
as if the breath
of a snowstorm will take them away.
And what to say about those houses:
They are hauling ghosts from another time.
It is easy to see pheasants walk in slumberous yards
with steps that show no rush.
You can see blacks with their privileges revoked,
whites preposterous about their color
walking by, face to face sometimes,
unaware of one another.
Detroit with its churches and voodoo,
fearful of God and the blues,
fearful of the truth.
He comes, goes, and dies in the hands of
a mortifier of flesh and souls.
One day He decided to visit a man
who left his church.
With chants, beseeched words, and promises of a
new beginning, He declared a holy war:
Love the World, He said.
I can't! the man answered.
Yes, you do! He defies. Here is my
blessing!
Love the world, He repeated.
The young man walked back to his house
to find a pheasant there, the pink velvet sofa,
the garages,
the houses,
the landscape is an arson.
Inside, he awakens
to wear the barren heart

given to him
when he was born
two thousand years before.

PARADE

Cities without
mountains
lives without
conscience
bodies without
desire
surround me.

The smell of the spring
is here
memories
of a childhood
of multicolored pansies
and hyacinths.

I feel happy for a second.

I walk the long corridor
until I touch
completely
the vision
of the green field of Chanco.

Here I see her,
her face in a duel with the sun.
I hear the music of a
summer parade.

I see my pink communion dress in her hands.

I do not know her smell.
Life has evolved.

Cities without
mountains
lives without
conscience
bodies without

desire
do not hurt
as much
as the cold heart
of my mother.

AMNESIA

Sometimes one forgets that
there do exist other mouths.
Sometimes one forgets that
there exist other meanings,
eyes, hands, bodies, codes,
that there exist other days,
other times,
the love of others.

One remembers
there exists much that one
would not want to forget.

Slowly they begin:
mouths,
eyes,
bodies,
codes,
others' love,
to seep through the walls
with Lucifer's subtlety,

and then one tries
to forget.

DO YOU REMEMBER LOVE?

Do you remember that summer day
when you and I followed the road to love?
I remember your lukewarm hand
between the pleats of my beige skirt.
Did you know that despite the years no one
had touched my thighs in such a way?
I wager you didn't know
how afraid I was
and at the same time how
anxious I was to be
alone with you.
I know that I cannot let you know how much
I have missed you since you left.
How can you find your
way back
if I erase these unbounded tracks?
In moments
when I live without you near
everything appears as illusion.
How can I let you know
that I still carry you with me
each step of my way,
that despite the passing of years,
I still feel your hand
between the pleats of my skirt.

HAIR OF SAND

From lost memory
it is getting closer.
Little by little,
half awake
and full of dust
comes
my mother tongue
to bring me
timid words,
whispers of a man in
my ear,
bells in an open sea,
winds from the south and white lilies.

It comes
charged with a nostalgia
to leave me a
package of rainy days,
warm bodies
in front of a fireplace.
It comes calm
with its hair of sand,
its mouth of ocean,
its caresses
in the dark.

It comes and says its verses
to calm my sadness.
It comes sweet and strong
with syllables I recognize,
its delicious sounds
with voices like a stream,
it comes and I in homage
as to a queen in her palace
I give her my precious
treasures
and subjugate myself, a slave
under her domain.

THE MOMENT OF TRUTH

I like you like that, full of imperfections, with that
indescribable hair that is not blond, black, or reddish,
with that big sharp nose
that cuts that Bremen face,
with those large and clumsy fingers
that hang like traps for my kisses,
with those grimaces born
suddenly from your mouth
with an accent that humiliates
my senses,
the baldness that
slowly shows,
that poignant tongue,
arrogant, full of sins,
hard like stone, venomous,
with a constant doubt
that to my heart emerges
with your frown of metaphor,
the blink of your
impatient eyes,
that look of whirlwinds
that open unknown caves,
that dissolve into subterranean places
to become fresh rain that will touch the
Black Forest and
wash away tears
fallen far too late.
I like you like that:
sometimes in calm
sometimes in revolt
with a sadistic anger that your
departure provoked,
with the illusion of seeing two bodies
that run to the immense summit
of mountains to touch,
to caress, to remember, to forgive,
rise up, venerate, approach,
to surpass themselves and resist forgetting,

then strip themselves their defects of pride until
finally they love each other.

I like you even though it hurts,
fugitive, thief of dreams,
beggar of truths,
echo of the messenger
of solitude, of occult pain, of green fields
where my red tears
will cover your plains.

I like you as far as Jupiter,
a thousand times back and forth.

And if suddenly someone sees me and
doesn't understand the reason for your power
it is because that someone never has loved
and has never been seduced by the
intoxicating light that
inundates the space where I live and
die every day a victim of
your magic constellation.
That someone never has seen your eyes or
the torrent of secret desires that inflame my veins
when your loud melodious laughter
opens the doors of the sky
and flourishes from my blindness this light
that I awaited in the dark.

LOVE IN TIME OF WAR

We have left a joy pending.
It was left in between hills and valleys
of this combatant people.

Don't stop firing now,
don't stop fighting,
we still have many years left
to reach our goal.

My inner voice says
the same thing every day.
I don't listen, I survive
day by day,
I don't worry any more about
the dreams of having you always close,
of knowing you always mine,
until it is too late and the hand of death takes
you with her.

Don't let strange voices confuse you about
what you already know.
Live, love, and fight with the same fervour of those
who know that life at any moment can go extinct.

THE DEW

I would like to see again a
dawn.

Do you remember
when the sand crept
into the sleeping bag
among our clothes?

Do you remember
what a fresh happiness
that was?

JEALOUS STATE

It was the Swedish fall when he came
with his coquettish hands, with his Holly Cole CD's,
a bunch of books in his bags,
a bottle of vodka for my birthday,
his legacy of a German soldier's son,
a pair of scissors to cut his hair,
like a Samson who wants to die.

He came among many others in the Scandinavian nights,
slowly and smiling,
dragged his tears and love behind.

He woke up sleeping the love of centuries,
volcanoes and butterflies appeared in my dreams,
I was quiet and shaken,
refusing to understand
life it's movements,
its mysteries.

I wanted to forget strange languages,
the time alone.
To hear happy "Waltzing Matilda"
And no more "Cold Ground."
He came impure and seductive,
he took my heart as his prize
he went back during the winter,
he left me behind to die.

UNEXPECTED DEATH

You will always be the absent
militant,
a lover that left,
a dead friend,
fallen compatriot.

Always, but for others.

For me, you will be
the paper notes hanging
on the door,
a dance of la Tirana,
or one of Mercedes Sosa's records,
especially the song about letting it all hang out,
a handshake,
a clandestine embrace,
a head that will be missing on
my pillows,
a chocolate ice cream at
Chez Henry,
going to the cinema in
Plaza Italia.

Do you remember?

You will be there in each
little hole in the wall,
in the white ceilings of
every house,
in the picture of the one
that sang "Flor de aromo,"
in our stolen Santiago,
in a candlestick of clay,
in the beautiful sign for
volunteer workers that says:

"Here lives the most beautiful couple in the world,
DO NOT DISTURB".

In the memory of the night.

You will always be
in the final commentary on Cortázar's Libro de Manuel,
and not knowing the "little bear" of the gigantic genius,
the one that the hydra took away.
It would be as if you were dead,
but not quite that simple.

It would be as if you left,
with boots on,
not with your own, my love,
but with mine.

BOYS

> "A torturer does not redeem himself through suicide.
> But it does help."
> – Mario Benedetti

The boys from the neighborhood, some of them,
stay behind the mud and the rain.

I ask myself what has become of
Romero, Quezada, Coleman?
Did their bodies and souls
escape deterioration?

Did they go into the army
to do their duty as soldiers
of the fatherland, the ones
who protect us from hate and
foreign tyrants?

Did they climb like the General
by usurping through disloyalty,
lies, secret codes and money?

Did they have families and
continue living in the city
as if nothing had happened?

Or did they sell their modest houses,
move to another neighborhood
where no one knows anything about them?

There they will come in the evening
to will wash the remnants of blood
from their fingers.

Will they look for their wives,
give them a kiss, touch them
with those same hands?

Will their daytime nightmares

be cast upon those who
know nothing of where they
come at the end of the night?

Will they return their heads,
smashed by the memories they left
in the cells, streets, apartments to a soft warm
pillow that washes away their sins?

What happened to the men
I knew and never saw again?

Did they turn themselves into
men hungry for justice or
did they leave little by little in silence?

Did they put on their clothes
in the morning without knowing
whether they would return in
the evening to their dear ones?

Did they learn to kill in clandestine training or
did they become more manly with the
passing of these hard times?

Did they love like those
pure boys
I met on those evenings
when to play was
our universe?

MEN OF FLESH AND BLOOD

For Jack Lessenberry

I have lived among men of flesh and blood.
I have loved, hated,
fought against
men of flesh and blood.

I have been conquered, humiliated,
I have been cast out to a shameful exile
among men of flesh and blood.
I have lost my home and my warm winter trappings.
I have emptied a thousand times the caverns of my torment.
I have forgotten in the daylight
the faces of my loved ones.
I have come back in the darkness to encountering them.
I have kept silent the name of God in my lament.

How can so much life run out in my absence without
knowing ?
I became a lonely tyrant of memories
of an ungraceful past.
I put behind that world with no regret, with no obsessions.
I'm careful with men of flesh and blood.
I'm not deceived by the quiet whispering of the wind,
by the music of the crickets,
by a red breasted robin in the blue summer of new encounters,
by the cold nights of winter
where the panic comes and goes like a soundless scream.
I'm afraid to raise my eyes to meet other eyes
to smile with my fallen mouth at other mouths.
I am heavenly distant from men of flesh and blood.

LOSS

What would you tell me if I asked you why?
Would you say nothing has changed?
Would you close the door if it
opens all the secrets of the past?
Why are you disappearing into the galaxy?
Why don't you believe any more in my invitations?

CHRISTMAS

Still I see your pale face in the dark
and the cold night of winter.

I remember the snowflakes
encrusted in your hair.
the car full of
books,
plants,
memories.

The freezing mornings or the heat of summer
fill my days.

Only sometimes when
I remember your quiet face,
knowing something I don't want to know,
I become anxious.

Nothing has changed since that Christmas.
Still I wait for you.

PRAYER

Tell me if you want someone.
Bring forward the obscure desires of
your shore in your body.
Conspire with me constantly about your dreams
where the sparks are
green and blue,
red and copper.

Allow me to hear you curse death.
Harvest my heart like a pomegranate
melting in your mouth.
Don't wake me up
if I fall asleep in your arms,
one, a dozen, hundreds of times.

Whisper in my mouth words in my native
tongue and rescue me from this
shellshock of years.

Read to me voices of the past.
Forget about new warrior poets
who have lost their sight.
Walk with me on the surface of
this earth. Unite your fingers
and your mouth with mine.

Let it be me who coddles your groomed head
on a white pillow. Trust the
undulating pulse of this day.

WHAT A SHAME

What a shame that all who used to talk so much
are here no more.

What a horror to have lost
everyone in pieces.

What a disgusting life
to have to continue
in purgatory.
How disgusting to have
reasons for a kiss.

What nonsense to still
have ears for a song,
lust for a cigarette,
what a shame to desire to give
a slap to a foreigner.

Why can't I throw stones
through the windows?
Why can't I pull
the claws off a lion?
Why is my energy gone
with a glass of vodka?

SAFE CONDUCT

> "And the crack in the tea-cup opens a lane to the land of the dead"
> –W.H. Auden

Who can imagine in one second
or in one moment
what exile produced in the
spirit of those expatriates?

Can anyone imagine
how those
bitter mouths, fallen, defeated,
tired of the fight with guttural
sounds, nasal
sounds that don't mean
anything in the ear to those who
pronounce them,
sounds that echo in the brain
looking for images
conceived in urgency, in
shame, in unknown ways,
in foreign countries.

How the pain is transformed
from a knot in the throat to a
violent fire in the stomach, to an
endless palpitating of a heart
that after surviving
senseless wars
is not used to the idea
that indifference
soaks the universe?

I ask myself if my mother
thought about me when
her fingers touched my picture
taken twenty years ago when
we still had tenderness,
if she shed a tear

when those same fingers
opened one of my letters,
if my friends
remembered my name when
celebrating their birthdays
if they sense that one of them
- me, the one that left -
is looking in their memory for
a way of meeting their
faces in the fog of distance.

How would I explain now,
that in a lonely night without
stars, in a place whose name I don't remember,
my heart pounding and my coquettish and seductive mind
hungry for life,
grasping blindly the smell
of *Diegos de la Noche*, the magic smells that exude
from their clothes and a penetrating halo
to the one I don't resist,
a flapping of the ocean that touches my feet
with its white fingers,
my iron will
disappears
slowly like
ashes over the ocean
and at a
whisper of *Ich liebe dich*
my solitary and tired spirit
succumbs to the enchantment of a sweet and
dangerous craziness?

RETURN

How does one take out
of the body
the feeling of this night?

How does one end the search
for the bird thief
that took the promise?
How does one remove the desire
from the raindrops?

Come.
I want to recognize your breath,
I want to remove the cobwebs of the centuries,
which have made silent the silence.

How does one excavate the earth
and know where to find you?

How does one open the skies
to know if you are there?

How do I open your grave
and remove your beautiful skull?
How do I enwrap it and protect it
from the cover of night?

How do I cleanse your eyes
of the dirt?
How do I open your mouth
to give you relief?
How do I close your eyes
they left open?
How do I make the wind
understand to take you little by little
but to have compassion for me?

How do I pray to God that He let me
return without you?

SUNSPOTS

The monster of the dark
abyss
resounds
like
bells
in your
absence.

There is no escape possible
to memories
that perfume with love
this dry earth.

The nights here are long.
In the passing of the years
the grief does not disappear.

My eyes
are lost in the becalmed
raft of your look.

My love,
I say goodbye.
Turn your head
slowly away.

Rest in peace.

I live now
in the fog of blinding lights.
Like resolana
I carry you on my skin.

ALONG THE COLD STREETS OF SCANDINAVIA

Along the cold streets of
Scandinavia
your Bremen silhouette between
trees and monuments
is hidden.
In a mantle of spring
you approach slowly
step by step
bit by bit
day by day.

Love that has been asleep for centuries
turns from colors of grey
to fuchsia, green,
blue, orange,
yellow, lilac,
the red of living sap.

I want to silence the silences.
I want to capture the exit
of those who have not yet
died but do not live in life.
I want to touch your
deep blue mind,
to rescue you,
to save myself
from those evenings of immunity,
from such foreign tongues,
from sterile exile.
I have wanted to change the world,
your world,
from your springs,
to empty with my dry mouth
the torrent of your waters.

I have wanted to remain
exhausted and soft
from the oceans, skies,

the red living sap,
to remain
awaiting
your sweet kiss,
the light touch
of your hand,
to wait naive
like a country girl
understanding
that what I understand is a lie,
that you will always be close by
whispering what I want to hear.

HUSBAND

Teach me to love you.
Take my hand and share with me
the light I see in your eyes.
Let me take shelter in your heart.
Let the door of the night open for me to stay or run.
Whisper to me your thoughts when I am distant
so I can come back to you, every day, every year,
every time.
Forgive my foolish heart for its mistakes.
Do not go back to that limbo where
we both came from.
Give me time to arise from the earth
and grow up as an oak with new roots,
tied to your roots like our legs in our nuptial bed.
Remember?
Let us braid our hearts because we want to.
Feel how I feel.
Allow me to be at peace with myself.
Let me come back slowly as the Maipo River
with its crazy sound.
Let me imagine cities with mountains
that we will walk up and down together again.
Bring to the sunroom of our house
a white chair,
a patient chair,
for I am here to stay

DEATH POSTPONED

Last night came death
to visit me with a thousand candles.
It came naked and cold
the way death always comes.

She told me she had
warm bedding and a suite
where I can
rest my agony.

She extended her cold hand
and whispered in my ear
No regrets, no reproaches,
she told me she will wait
at each corner,
in each forest,
behind every sight.

Here she comes
to take me without my dresses,
without rags, without shyness,
to take me to her castle
without moons,
to her horizons without hills.

I wake up in a start
till Death departs angrily
and promises to come back.

I am like the knight of La Mancha.
Never die! Never die!
It is the motto I carry on my chest,
that I hang up on the fence
outside my house
at the beginning
of each night.

WOLF

For Mauricio Arenas Bejas.

The last time I saw you I left
with the sensation that we would meet again much later.

You entered into my life a bit unwelcome.
Because of your tone, you understand.

When I realized how
lonely you were
I was more calm,
my loneliness would not be
something I would have to hide.
You and I were of the same kind.

When I think of you now, I become shaken,
I have questions,

everything inconclusive, like our encounters.

Despite everything it was a good time,
we were alive, full of sun and fears.

How can I forget your
beautiful black eyes?

Maybe I should have gone to the lakes in the South,
to breathe clean air. I didn't dare.
I feel bad when I think
of this. I left you alone.
It wasn't like you needed company but
if I would have gone it would
have been the close of another inconclusive story.

I know that you were right.
It is senseless to ask
myself questions about
such encounters.

Maybe despite everything I
can promise you a morning walk in the park,
or you can give me a hand when they come looking for me,
when the hurricane strikes again.
We have to believe that they cannot eliminate us,
or at least that they can't defeat us.

I always thought that
I should have known you before, when you were little.

Despite knowing much about you,
you were one of those solitary creatures of whom
one never knows much, those who come to be great,
but in life are much ignored.

Today I read an article in the newspaper.
How it pains me that you are hurt.

For more than a year I wished
it wasn't you.
I thought it was a confusion of names.
You were hurt like the others,
what bad luck.
I always thought of you,
of what we did,
when you were angry with me,
the time was short but you
stayed there
in permanent memories.

For me everything has been different.
I live groping
in empty exile that perhaps one day
will only be an unpleasant memory
on foreign ground.

The world falls down around me with the death of my
companion. Maybe you can understand me a little bit.
Today my heart is broken, anguished with the death of
so many of ours.

You remember the last time
we met?
I don't.
Sometimes I confuse the
circumstances of the past with the sinister present.

Perhaps we can meet again one day
by the light of day, of summer, of fresh
ideas, of an end to this
loneliness.
A day that I await
with a heart purely in hope of bringing
to Chile all that is good once more.

Uppsala, 1991

HOW CHAOS BEGINS

A butterfly flying in the streets
of Santiago
on a September day.

OLD MOUNTAINS

I ask myself what I would say
if you were to enter my door
at this very moment.

If you could lift the iron gate
of your coffin
and walk through the hemisphere
from south to north
just to find me.

I would ask you:
What have you been doing
the past twenty years?

I would invite you for black tea or
chocolate ice cream
and with the same yellow old shoes
we would walk through our city
and wet old mountains
to relive every single step
of our past
until we would collapse
in showers of laughter.

I probably would cry too,
not of sadness
but of the glad feeling
that will grow inside me
and explode like a helium balloon
in my eyes.

I would believe in miracles then.

SONG FOR CHILE

So many days of restlessness
between the bars of the forgotten.

So many kisses and furtive embraces
that turn grey and disappear into the universe.

Thousands of sweet melodies.

Images full of horror sometimes, others full of furies.
Words that enclose our destinies,
our dreams, this craziness.

Words that symbolize the
precious
meaning of our existence
become bubbles
suddenly
one morning.

The colors of dusk declining in the West of the universe,
the dark red of fright and hope.

All that I love close and in the distance.
Everything gone to a tiny remote place,
where you appear
five seconds each day.

I carry you like a white perfumed shirt,
that brings me
pride and praises.
I take you,
caress you,
and hide you
in my sacred ritual,
where you will come
to relieve me of pain,
to help me in this
disillusionment.

Return to me fresh as the time before this evil covered us.
I will keep you close and protected
the way you did
before evil covered us.
I will polish you
five seconds every dawn.

I will clothe you
in fine colors that
will illuminate the distance.

RIPPLES

I enter the daylight like a vampire
ready to suck the last drop of the dew
spread on the green grass of August.

I enter afraid of new sounds
of the morning, scratching the silences of this room.

In a corner, I see my grandfather
in the old country drinking tea for breakfast
in the kitchen.
He is striding
robust, with no fears,
back and forth,
moving his hands on a soft
loaf of bread.

Through the window, sun
emerges defiant through mountains
full of secrets and gossip from the city.

He moves towards the light,
walks to the door, leaving behind
the key to a mandala.
He is a soft flapping ticking
in my ears,
the heart
of a little girl waiting
for his return.

VALENTINE'S DAY IN DETROIT

The sounds of children playing in the snow,
a bunch of orange roses and a sign
"Be my Valentine"
on the round surface of this day.

Are these moments similar
to the ones we dreamt of?
We couldn't answer, we are not others.
We are the ones standing still,
almost faceless.

Here we are inventing words
on this hammock despite
the baby spit.

A house untied to the ground,
a laundry room of nostalgias,
a window clouded by
little sleep,
a coat of memories we remove
every February,
a simple grin and a Sanders chocolate box,
then, we grow to the light like sweet peas.

CYANIDE SMILE

It is a crime that violates no law.

I learned it well at home
with Grandmother.

She hid her smile to use against us.

So powerful, so invisible,
that sword.

She knew if she used it
in small doses
she would find us like lambs.

She knew its power on small scale.

Even war is not so cruel.

INSOMNIA

Today I recover you.
I breathe the air that I breathe
without making myself cry.

I pulled you out and I lick your memory
like a dog,
from the tip of your toes to
your hair.
It pained me to the marrow
knowing you are dead.
I don't know where
the calm and the stillness reside.
I know you are there in some
corner of the universe,
in the picture of our little rabbit,
a memory falling from the roof.

How can I walk slowly when
I go to meet you?

How can I go back and relive everything
when there is nothing left?

There are many questions that accost me in exile.
The day starts to break.
I have to say goodbye.
You have to go back to your place
so I can continue to live
this paradox of light and
shadows.

GREED

Did you fail my love on purpose?
Did you run away from
yourself to shame your soul?

Did your face shed a tear when you thought about me?

A thousand are my unanswered questions.
A thousand are my *saudades* for you.
Not everything worked the way we wanted.

The city was filled with music of the war,
the demons hidden behind dresses and sonatas that came
looking for you.

You were Narcissus in front of the mirror
trying to locate your face in my body.

Do you cry?
I don't want to see tears in those eyes.

Distance is only temporary.

We still can fool your
consciousness and leave judgment to others.

We can still look each other
in the eye and smile.
We still fool ourselves about your soul and mine.

SOMETIMES

Sometimes I miss
a little bit of happiness,
a transparent glance
that transforms
the bitter routine
of my days,
fall leaves that move with the wind
when they hit the ground.

I miss
a long night
full of generosity
and laziness.
One of your kisses
falls upon my breast,
a tender caress
touching my hair
and a new whispering
gives back
the illusion
of not having lost you.

My heart cries
at knowing you are so far,
so strange,
of knowing you eternal.

Tell me that it is only a moment
that you will be gone,
even if I know it is a lie.

I miss
a little bit of happiness.
Sometimes
the space on my pillow
tells me
I am missing you.

ABSOLUTION

For Marisela Conejeros

When the call of the rooster
awakens me once again in the morning,
and the dark red of dusk
enters through my pupils and doesn't hurt my heart,
when my voice can pronounce
again his name
and the ground that I walk upon cannot be so hard and cold
and winter disappears,
when your children and my children can play
all day without brawls,
and the sounds of the street are all recognizable and clear, not
    foreign,
you and I can look into each other's eyes
and discover that we still can smile,
when you come looking for me and need
to know if I am there,
I will tell you that I've never left,
that I have always been here waiting
for an encounter, a tear that
will fall down your cheek to wash away forever
the misery of having lost him.

April 10, 2001

BROKEN GLASS

I don't understand where I left my weapons:
I only know, and of this I am sure,
I will find the thread of this road
that I left to walk those perpetual
horizons.

Dreams and
ambitions lost
in many graves.
in the silent goodbyes
of Chileans.

With dry eyes and no tears left,
they took almost everything and left me half sleepy,
claiming compassion in a low voice,
so that the earth doesn't
swallow me.

The truce has been long and yet I am not over it.
My hands were left mutilated
by empty bodies.
The scars run deep.
I don't regret anything.
I only prepare my vengeance.
Moment by moment.
And in secret.

TWINKIES

A fallen apple is on our hungry table.
You don't see it but I do.
You kiss me goodbye and let me go.
Here alone with a fallen apple close to my mouth
I try not to see its orange rays
defy my eyes.
It's fragrant like an orchard
when the fall is ripe.
I try to move my lips,
comb my hair,
clean my house,
powder my nose,
be philosophical and lie,
be little affected by the fear of others,
care about prizes and money,
dress in a suit of conventional life and
with my exceptional eyes
blink when I open my door.
Smile to those who have been lifting
the skirts of their colleague's wives,
deceived themselves once, dozens, hundreds   f of times,
talk to those who kept you company.
I tried, really, to be superior, enlightened
by no fear but I didn't succeed.
It was then that I took off
my coat of pride and doubt.
"Don't leave me alone, I beg you," I meant to say
as if the words could
come out like a stampede from my mouth.
"I don't find the way to explain
such an urgency, such a complicated task."
You will say:"It is not there,
it is just me with too much time on my hands.
There is nothing to be afraid of, it is an empty
wooden table and it is completely dry."
The days are falling, months
passing by.

I'm alone at my hungry table with
a fallen apple in my mouth.

ARCADE

The same man mourning
will no longer see me as I was
but who I will become.

The mirror where you find
my face will become the pale flat destiny
that earth planned for us.

Why does the silence keeps those secrets silent
so man passes confused in death and lust?

FROM THE GRAVES OF LATIN AMERICA

Before I jump into the abyss
searching for you
and with a broken voice pronounce your name,
before the world drowns
in the darkness again,
remember my love and don't tremble,
here will be an eternal rest,
not one leaf will be moved by
the wind to give us relief.
We will be immobile before the silence
of the world
and the ignoble serenity of cemeteries.
We will stay
you and I alone
in the profundity
of your grave,
the night and its silence.

DETROIT

When I drive down from
Grosse Pointe on Warren
a sudden knot in my heart
is born.

Solitude
is roaming
with the images of
a city broken
and gone.

I cross my fingers
hoping I won't see
any black cats
crossing
these steaming manholes.

Detroit, so full of churches,
so where is God?

Could He be hiding
under politicians' coats?

A "mon cher"
looked through my car window
and believed
he melted snow.

His eyes aflame
consumed two seconds
when the red light stopped.

City in flames,
who took away your palaces?

It was not me.
I am a foreigner,
I just came to see.

Detroit, wake up
from your sleep.

Rebuild your empire.
Rebuild it
so I can see.

Forget about
black LaKeishas
and your white Portias.
Forget about your yellow Chengs
and your brown Carolas.

Let the golden haze
that rusts on your aura
shine proudly
on your face again.

Let a feeling of goodness
drench the city like a storm.
Let your dreams flourish and endure.
Turn the holy fight into
salutation.
Let the happiness return.
Leave your vinegar grief behind.

Let me see, Detroit.
Let me see.

Biography of Mariela Griffor

Mariela Griffor was born in the city of Concepción in southern Chile. She attended the University of Santiago and the Catholic University of Rio de Janeiro. Griffor left Chile for an involuntary exile in Sweden in 1985. She and her American husband returned to the United States in 1998 with their two daughters. They live in Grosse Pointe Park, Michigan. She is co-founder of The Institute for Creative Writers at Wayne State University and Publisher of Marick Press. Her work has appeared in periodicals across Latin America and the United States. Griffor holds a B.A in Journalism and an M.A. in Communications from Wayne State University. She is a Joel oppenheimer Scholar at New England College. She is Honorary Consul of Chile in Michigan. Griffor is the author of *Exiliana* and *House*.

ARS INTERPRES PUBLICATIONS

World poetry in English translation and English language poetry

In 2004 we began publishing bilingual books of poetry with English-Russian editions of Les Murray and John Kinsella. The series continues to grow.
Forthcoming books include the work of: Antoni Albalat (Catalan-English), Jóhann Hjálmarsson (Icelandic-English), Per Wästberg, (Swedish-English-Russian), as well as a Swedish-English anthology of contemporary Swedish poets.

NEW IN AUTUMN 2006

Ewa Lipska, *The Holy Order of Tourists*

"This is poetry I love but if asked why, in fact I would have to say it defies classification." — *Stanislaw Lem*

Daniel Weissbort, *The Name's Progress*

"It's hard to imagine how anything could be more natural, relaxed and true to the writer's self, true to his secret, personal life, than Daniel Weissbort's poems." — *Ted Hughes*

John Kinsella, *America or Glow*

"He has improvised an Australian epic lyric by lyric, book by book...moving forward unaggressively yet momentously, like a geological process." — *Publishers Weekly*

Visit us at www.arsint.com

www.ingramcontent.com/pod-product-compliance
Lightning Source LLC
LaVergne TN
LVHW011430080426
835512LV00005B/358